Kiss the Son

... a fresh perspective on how to serve the king

ADEKUNLE OBE

Order this book online at www.trafford.com/09-0361
or email orders@trafford.com

Most Trafford titles are also available at major online book retailers.

Note for Librarians: A cataloguing record for this book is available from Library and Archives Canada at www.collectionscanada.ca/amicus/index-e.html

ISBN: 978-1-4269-0782-1

www.trafford.com

North America & international
toll-free: 1 888 232 4444 (USA & Canada)
phone: 250 383 6864 • fax: 250 383 6804 • email: info@trafford.com

The United Kingdom & Europe
phone: +44 (0)1865 487 395 • local rate: 0845 230 9601
facsimile: +44 (0)1865 481 507 • email: info.uk@trafford.com

10 9 8 7 6 5 4 3 2 1

Contents

Dedication

I dedicate this book to the glory of:

God Almighty, my heavenly father,

Lord Jesus Christ, my Savior and

The Holy Spirit, my helper, and inspiration.

Preface

Kiss the Son, my second book after my first: The Pattern Son; is a collection of thoughts, inspirations, and impressions by the Holy Spirit.

The opinions, views expressed in this book (just like my first book) are from my own personal perspective.

I hope you will understand that I 'am just another earthen/clay (imperfect, human) vessel. -II Corinthians 4:7.

That's why, it is imperative to refer to the Scriptures, the only authoritative material and wait on the Holy Spirit, for understanding, the vehicle for ***knowing the only true God and Jesus Christ, whom He hast sent.***-John 17: 3.

I believe, Kiss the Son, will be an invaluable asset to anyone who wants to worship God and serve in his vineyard, kingdom.

I wish to recognize: Bro Samuel Olowoyo, for your invaluable assistance towards this book, and all those who have in one way or the other contributed towards the success of this project.

Moreover, and most importantly, you, who have decided to read this book.

The message about **Kiss the Son** will not have been complete without you.

ADEKUNLE OBE
Website: www.Jedidah.com
Email: info@jedidah.com

Introduction

Kiss the Son, lest he be angry, and ye perish from the way, when his wrath is kindled but a little. Blessed are all they that put their trust in him. -Psalm 2:12.

This book is about understanding some underlying truths for purposeful service in God's vineyard, through an intimate relationship with the Jesus Christ, **the Lord of lords and King of kings** -Revelations 17:14.

The primary reason for our existence is to worship God in Spirit and in truth, through an intimate fellowship with Him

It is only when our service is based/flowing from such intimacy/ relationship, that it can be classified as an act of true worship unto God.

Then saith Jesus unto him, Get thee hence, satan: for it is written, Thou shalt worship the Lord thy God, and him only shalt thou serve - Matthew 4:10.

Thou shalt fear the LORD thy God, and serve him... -Deuteronomy 6:13.

This is the foundation for our rulership and Dominion on the earth.

Under the Old Testament dispensation, believers in Jehovah could only serve Him as servants.

And Moses verily was faithful in all his house, as a servant, for a testimony of those things, which were to be spoken after; But Christ as a son over his own house: whose house are we, if we hold fast the confidence and the rejoicing of the hope firm unto the end. -Hebrews 3:5, 6.

Jesus Christ 'broke the ice' as the first person to serve God as a son.

Also, by his death, burial, resurrection and ascension to Heaven, he became the door and opened the way wherein, any man (those who would receive him as Lord and Savior) can now become sons of God and enjoy the privilege of obeying and honoring Him in service.

This is one of the uniqueness of the New Testament dispensation.

Even Angels do not have the privilege of serving God as sons.

And because ye are sons, God hath sent forth the Spirit of his Son into your the hearts, crying, Abba Father.
Wherefore thou art no more a servant, but a son; and if a son, then an heir of God through Christ -Galatians 4:6,7

Behold what manner of love the father hath bestowed upon us, that we should be called the sons of God: therefore the world knoweth us not, because it knew him not -I John 3:1.

Kissing the Son is to worship, adore, honor, obey, submit, surrender serve, and embrace God's ways on a daily basis as we prepare for the second coming of, God's chosen King, the Lord Jesus Christ.

Why do we have so much conflict, confusion and turbulence/destruction (political, social, etc) in the world/among the nations of the earth?

It is because Man has failed to exercise his power of Choice to Kiss the Son.

King David's prophetic declaration in *Psalms 2:1-12* is very instructive, especially in these our times.

He that is not with me is against me; and he that gathereth not with me scattereth abroad -Matthew 12:30.

Any man, community, tribe, country, or nation that fails to submit to the lordship of Jesus Christ stands the risk of incurring the wrath of God's judgment.

It is far better to 'kiss' the Son than to be 'killed' (destroyed) by the Son, when He comes back to judge all the people on the earth. Surely He will come and His coming is imminent.

In other words, purposeful and fulfilling living on the earth (no matter your race, color, background, beliefs or sex) is premised on your becoming God's child (through faith in the finished work of Jesus Christ, on the Cross of Calvary) and serving Him.

Our service in Christ's vineyard is one of the ways, in which we, as his children, can honor God.

A son honoreth his father, and a servant his master: If then I be a father, where is mine honour? and if I be a master, where is my fear? saith the LORD of hosts unto you... -Malachi 1: 6.

Do you want the Father's honor? Then serve Him, in obedience to His word.

If any man serve me, let him follow me; and where I am, there shall also my servant be: if any man serve me, him will my Father honor -John 12:26.

What an awesome honor to be called by Him!!!

What a great joy to belong to Him!!!

What a unique privilege to serve Him!!!

I hope you will be blessed as you enjoy reading this book.

However and more importantly, my prayer is that, as you read this book 'Kiss the Son', you will enter into a higher dimension of intimacy with God, which will enable you to serve Him better, in line with His plan and purposes for your life in Jesus name, Amen.

Your Co-laborer in His vineyard.

Adekunle Obe

Chapter 1

Flesh -Our Greatest Foe

O wretched man that I am! Who shall deliver me from the body of this death? Romans 7: 24.

Talk of an enemy within the door - that clearly depicts 'the body of this death': our flesh, a nature and the product of the fallen man.

It is the believer's greatest enemy and the major hindrance in our quest to serve the LORD.

We can identify the flesh as the unrenewed or yet to be renewed part of our **being**.

Here, specifically, **being** refers to our soul: will, attitudes, mindset; thought patterns, desires, tendencies/inclinations and values.

These, affect our decisions, approach to life, what we say and what we do. Because this conflict rages on in our soul, we can safely submit that our soul is the arena where the greatest battles of our life will take place.

In other words, our flesh is, whatsoever we put our confidence in, we can boast of, or take our sense of worth, value/significance from; other than God.

For we are the circumcision which worship God in the spirit and rejoice in Christ Jesus, and have no confidence in the flesh. Though I might also have confidence in the flesh, if any other man thinketh that he hath whereof he might trust in the flesh, I more: Circumcised the eighth day, of the stock of Israel, of the tribe of Benjamin, an Hebrew of the Hebrews; as touching the law, a Pharisee; Concerning zeal, persecuting the church; touching righteousness, which is in the law, blameless -Philippians 4: 3 - 6.

Here we see, that Paul's credentials, as stated in *verses 5 -6*, can be classified as of the flesh: our achievements, qualities, positions in the natural. Confidence in these things constitutes a hindrance to our true worship of God.

God is a Spirit: and they that worship him must worship him in spirit and in truth -John 4: 24.

Whenever, we start depending on the arm of the flesh, we are distracted from focusing on the Lord Jesus Christ.

This causes us to feel insecure and inferior: the root cause of all demonic onslaughts.

Our intrinsic value of who we are in Christ far surpasses anything we can ever have or achieve in life.

The value of any human being, redeemed by the precious blood of Jesus, cannot be compared to anything human or anything in the natural that we can glory in.

But God forbid that I should glory, save in the cross of our Lord Jesus Christ, by whom the world is crucified unto me, and I unto the world -Galatians 6: 14.

"Most failures in Ministries can be traced to a failure in the Minister's personal life (relationship with God, health, marriage, family and finances etc) as a result of not living a crucified life/walking in the Spirit, which is the only way to deal with our flesh."

The flesh is the root cause of idolatry, the breeding ground for religious spirits. God is a jealous God, who hates idolatry.

For thou shalt worship no other god: for the LORD, whose name is jealous, is a jealous God -Exodus 34:14.

Religion breeds "faith" in man made rituals, routine, ceremonies externalities and "unbelief" in true spirituality, which is a heart connection with God through the Lord Jesus Christ.

While religion leads to spiritual sickness, decay and death; a personal relationship (operating by faith) with Jesus, as Lord and Savior, brings healing/heath and ultimately, life.

Shrines, temples artifacts etc dedicated to 'saints' (every born again Christian is a saint) and religious practices become idolatrous whenever the focus is now on the object and not on the Lord Jesus Christ.

The anointing oil, a symbol of the Holy Ghost, could also be 'abused', if the focus is now on the oil and no more on the Lord Jesus Christ. The Holy Ghost is not oil, nor does He live in oil or in a bottle.

The anointing oil, ought to be used as a point of contact, as inspired by the Holy Ghost, and not as a magician's wand for getting a miracle.

Know ye not that ye are the temple of God, and that the Spirit of God dwelleth in you? -I Corinthians 3:16

Why would a Minister charge 'consultation' or 'appearance' fees before preaching the word? Is still God's servant, sent to His people or a performer in the world?

These twelve Jesus sent forth, and commanded them, saying, Go not into the way of the Gentiles, and not into any of the city of the Samaritans enter ye not, But go rather to the lost sheep of the house of Israel. And as ye go to the, preach, saying the kingdom of heaven is at hand. Heal the sick, cleanse lepers, raise the dead, and cast out devils: freely ye have received, freely give -Matthew 10:5-8.

Has he forgotten that, freely did God give him those abilities?
Why didn't God charge us for our salvation? If He did, who could have afforded it?

We need to watch our heart so that it is not corrupted by the 'subtle desire' of the flesh to be paid 'money for services rendered' under the disguise of collecting honorarium.

And he returned to the man of God, he and all his company, and came, and stood before him: and he said, Behold, now I know that there is no God in all the earth, but in Israel: now therefore pray thee, take a blessing of thy servant.
But he said, As the LORD liveth, before whom I stand, I will receive none. And he urged him to take it, but he refused -II kings 5:15,16.

Why did Elisha, the prophet, refuse Naaman's (captain of the host of the king of Syria) gifts? Because Naaman wanted to pay for his healing but God's healing is not, never for sale.

And he said unto him, Went not mine heart with thee, when the man turned again from his chariot to meet thee? Is it a time to receive money, and to receive garments, and olive yards, and vineyards, and sheep, and oxen, and menservants, and maidservants? -II kings 5:26.

From the above, we can also see that there is a time to receive gifts. However, we have to be spiritually minded to discern such times.

And Jesus went into the temple of God, and cast out all them that sold and bought in the temple, and overthrew the tables of the moneychangers, and the seats of them that sold doves. And said unto them, It is written, My house shall be called the house of prayer: but ye have made it a den of thieves. And the blind and the lame came to him in the temple; and he healed them -Matthew 21:12-14.

Dove symbolizes the anointing of the Holy Spirit. In other words, some have made merchandise of God's *anointing* on their lives.

Also, you will observe that Jesus had to clear the temple of such 'merchants', before real revival could happen.

Can we safely say that the reason why we do not have revival in our lives, churches and congregation is because; we have occupied our hearts with 'things' of this world rather than the 'things' of God?

We are the only ones who can answer such a question and make the necessary changes.

And Jesus said, Are ye also yet without understanding? Do not ye yet understand that whatsoever entereth in at the mouth goeth into the belly, and is cast out into the draught? But those things which proceed out of the mouth come forth from the heart; and they defile the man For out of the heart proceed evil thoughts, murders, adulteries, fornications, thefts, false witness, blasphemies: These are the things which defile a man: but to eat with unwashen hands defileth not a man -Mathew 15:16-20.

Yielding to the bidding of the flesh pollutes our heart, which is the manufacturing center of our thoughts, words and actions.

The fruit of this process are the works of the flesh.

Now the works of he flesh are manifest, which are these; Adultery, fornication, uncleanness, lasciviousness. Idolatry, witchcraft, hatred, variance, emulations, wrath, strife, seditions, heresies. Envyings, murders, drunkenness, revellings, and such like: of the which I tell you before, as I have also told you time past, that they, which do such things, shall not inherit the kingdom of God -Galatians 5: 19 - 21.

Also, negative behavior such as manipulation, gossip, intimidation, slander, arrogance/haughtiness, ridicule, pity party, threats, blame, nagging, and deception can be classified as acts of the flesh.

Ideas, thoughts, inspirations from our flesh may sound good but it cannot be godly. In fact such/some 'good' ideas become hindrances to godly ones.

While all good ideas may not be godly, all godly ideas are definitely, not just good, but are the best. The flesh factor is that which causes self-deception in our hearts and causes us to be inclined toward sin.

The heart is deceitful above all things, and desperately wicked: who can know it? -Jeremiah 17:9

This is the heart that has been overcome or polluted by the flesh. That's why God (and not our heart) is our ultimate guide whom we can safely trust.

This I say then, walk in the Spirit, and ye shall not fulfill the lust of the flesh, For the flesh lusteth against the Spirit, and the Spirit against the flesh: and these are contrary the one to the other: so that ye cannot do the things that ye would -Galatians 5:16, 17.

The flesh always seeks to pervert, distort and destroy the cause of the spirit. It cannot be 'mastered' or pampered, because it will still show its ugly 'face' in another area of our life.

Apostles Paul discissus this burning issue in Chapters 7 and 8 of the book of Romans.

Since 'Flesh' stinks, what can we do?

The solution is to live a Crucified life or simply put: walk in the Spirit.

For the law of the Spirit of life in Christ Jesus hath made me free from the law of sin and death -Romans 8:2.

Operating the higher law of the Spirit is the way out of this human dilemma.

For to be carnally minded is death; but to be spiritually minded is life and peace -Romans 8:6.

What does walking in the Spirit mean? It simply means trusting God, and living by faith in line with God's word.

Living by faith is exercising confidence in and acting on God's word (as a living productive, active reality that does/functions, just as it has been said/spoken or written down in scriptures) in our thoughts, words and actions.

As long as we are still living in this human body on planet earth, walking in the Spirit/living a crucified life, ought to be every Christian believer' lifestyle.

It is not only the antidote to our flesh but also a sure proof that we profess the faith we believe in.

I am crucified with Christ: nevertheless I live; yet not I, but Christ liveth in me: and the life which I now live in the flesh (flesh here refers to our body), I live by the faith of the Son of God, who loved me, and gave himself for me. -Galatians 2: 20

And they that are Christ's have crucified the flesh with the affections and lusts -Galatians 5:24.

Living a Crucified life will entail 'suffering' in the flesh: self-denial, discipline. This is true Christian 'suffering', not the kind of suffering as understood by the world(which is an absence of God in a situation or environment)

Suffering, from the Christian perspective, is the presence of God/God's approval in whatever adverse circumstance we may find ourselves

But I keep under my body, and bring it into subjection: lest that by any means, when I have preached to others, I myself should be castaway. -I Corinthians 9:27.

I believe that Apostle Paul, in using the word "my body", wasn't just referring to his physical body but the desires, cravings of his soul (which manifest, eventually, through our body), which if not controlled, can 'pollute' us or derail us from God's purposes/doing things God's way.

This is true 'self mastery': subduing/bringing our emotions, feelings, and tendencies etc, with the help of the Holy Spirit, into conformity to the will of God.

Crucifying our flesh is a conscious act of our will (decisions, resolve, and determination); we die to self by yielding to, obeying God.

But put ye on the lord Jesus Christ, and make not provision for the flesh, to fulfill the lusts thereof -Romans 13:14.

It will involve us, yielding to the law of the Spirit of life in Christ Jesus, which is the antidote to the law of sin and death (already in operation in our flesh, adamic nature).

There is therefore now no condemnation to them, which are in Christ Jesus, who walk not after the flesh, but after the Sprit. For the law of the Spirit of life in Christ Jesus hath made me free from the law of sin and death -Romans 8:1, 2.

Walking in the Spirit is the only way we can please God, our father.

Ministry, in fact, the Christian faith, is all about doing His will. This is what guarantees us spending eternity with Him. Whether you are a preacher or layman, there are adverse repercussions, if we fail to walk in the Spirit.

The flesh: the destroyer of destinies

Our Scriptural passage, in this area, is taken from *I Samuel 21:1-9* and *I Samuel 22:6-23.*

In this story, we see Doeg the Edomite (symbolizing the flesh), the chiefest of the herd men that belonged to Saul (a type of the Devil).

He is the One who discloses the hospitality that Ahimelech (symbolizing the carnal believer or a believer that accommodates the flesh) accorded to David (symbolizing the spiritual man/believer).

He is also the person who carries out the heinous crime of murdering the priests of Nob.

Now a certain man of the servants of Saul was there that day, detained before the LORD; and his name was Doeg, an Edomite, the chiefest of the herdmen that belonged to Saul -I Samuel 21:7.

Then answered Doeg the Edomite, which was set over the servants of Saul, and said, I saw the son of Jesse coming to Nob, to Abimelech the son of Ahitub. And he enquired of the LORD for him and gave him victuals, and gave him the sword of Goliath the Philistine I Samuel 22: 9, 10.

The flesh has no respect for spiritual matters. Doeg went ahead to kill the priests of the LORD, even though the other servants of Saul refused.

And the king said, Thou shalt surely die, Ahimelech, Thou, and all thy father's house. And the king said unto the footmen that stood about him, Turn, and slay the priests of the LORD; because they knew when he fled, and did not shew it to me. But the servants of the king would not put forth their hand to fall upon the priests of the LORD -I Samuel 22:16, 17.

The destructive nature of the flesh goes beyond 'reasonable' barriers. Doeg went beyond Saul's instruction to kill Ahimelech, and his father's entire house.

And Nob the city of the priests, smote he with the edge of the sword, men and women, children and sucklings and oxen, and asses, and sheep, with the edge of the sword -I Samuel 22:18.

We should recognize the fact that one of Satan's strategies is to use, 'our' flesh, as an instrument of death to destroy us and others.

And David said unto Abiathar, I knew it that day, when Doeg the Edomite was there, that he would surely tell Saul have occasioned the death of all the persons of thy father's house -I Samuel 22:22.

Whenever we start functioning in the flesh; we are out of God's purpose, and are vulnerable to the world and the god of this world - Satan and his demons.

In fact, Satan only gets a legal right into our lives if we walk in the flesh and not in the spirit.

Hereafter will not talk much with you: for the prince of this world (the devil) cometh, and hath nothing in me -John 14:30.

Nothing here includes anything that belongs to or is associated with the flesh - fallen nature.

This is the testimony of Jesus, when the devil came to 'check him out'.

Jesus walked fully in the Spirit during his time on the earth.

Be not deceived; God is not mocked: for whatsoever a man soweth, that shall he also reap. For he that soweth to his flesh shall of the flesh reap corruption; but he that soweth to the Spirit shall of the Spirit reap life everlasting. -Galatians 6: 7,8.

"The Christian faith is not about Giftings or Manifestations of the Spirit (though it includes such) but is premised on our Continual Walk of Faith with the Master, Jesus Christ - Walking in the Spirit".

We should not be like the Galatian church; to whom Apostle Paul wrote:

O foolish Galatians, who hath bewitched you, that ye should not obey the truth, before whose eyes Jesus Christ hath been evidently set forth, crucified among you? This only would I learn of you, Received ye the Spirit by the works of the law, or by the hearing of faith?
Are ye so foolish? Having begun in the Spirit, are ye now made perfect by the flesh? -Galatians 3: 1 - 4.

At the new birth, our spirit man is instantly recreated. Being born-again, not of corruptible seed, but of incorruptible, by the word of God, which liveth and abideth forever -I Peter 1:23.

Therefore if any man be in Christ, he is a new creature: old things are passed away; behold, all things are become new -II Corinthians 5: 17.

That's why we are instructed by God, speaking through Apostle Paul, in *Romans 12:1* not to be conformed to this world: but be ye transformed by the renewing of your mind, that ye may prove what is good, and acceptable, and perfect, will of God.

Receiving the end of your faith, even the salvation of your soul
-II Peter 1:9.

In *John 10:10,* We receive Zoe 'Life' at the new birth but we can only enjoy and partake of abundant life when we undergo 'process', God's dealings in our lives, and consciously subject ourselves to the discipline of the faith.

Let us watch and guard against anything or act that can take our focus from the lord Jesus Christ; for God will not share His glory (worship, acknowledgement, praise, adoration) with any man.

Not every one that saith unto me, Lord, lord, shall enter into the kingdom of heaven; but he that doeth the will of my Father, which is in heaven. Many will say to me in that day, Lord, lord, have we not prophesied in thy name? and in thy name done many wonderful works? And then will I profess unto them, I never knew you: depart from me, ye that work iniquity -Matthew 7:21 -23.

From the above, it can be clearly seen that Prophesy and doing wonderful works may not be full proof that a person is doing God's will.

How is this possible? If we walk in the flesh by:

(a) Not walking in Christ Love: serving God out of ungodly motives, attitudes.

(b) Indulging in unauthorised works: works not initiated or sanctioned/approved by the Holy Spirit.

(c) Using carnal, worldly methods, instead of God's methods, for serving the King.

We can see the story of Israel in *I Chronicles 13:1-14*, when they tried to bring the ark of God back to Israel by using an heathen method, (a new cart, which attracted God's displeasure rather than His blessing) instead of God's prescribed way.

"Worldly methods, rather than bring the glory of God, will attract God's judgment".

While we may have right intentions, it does not justify us if we do the things of God in our own way. We ought to still seek God's face so that we can serve him in His own way.

Remember God is a jealous God who prefers us doing things in His own way.

Compare with Chapters 15 and 16 of I Chronicles, when Israel did the right thing the right way.

And said unto them, Ye are the chief of the fathers of the Levites: sanctify yourselves, both ye and your brethren, that ye may bring up the ark of the LORD God of Israel unto the place that I have prepared for it. For because ye did it not at the first, the LORD our God made a breach upon us, for that we sought him not after the due order -I Chronicles 15:12,13.

(d) Self sent: 'sending' yourself when God has not sent you or calling yourself into Ministry when God hasn't called you.

"We do not volunteer (ask God) to be Ministers of the gospel, God asks for us."

According to Jesus, many Christians will fall into this trap of deception, where they will be Operating in the flesh and still believe that they were doing the Father's will.

My sincere prayer, is that on that last day, none of us will be found, in this 'many' category Jesus talked about in Matthew 7:21-23;in Jesus name, Amen.

The Independent Spirit

An 'independent spirit' is a worldly spirit emanating from satan, which manifests through the works of the flesh. It thrives and aspires to a state where Man is 'independent' of God - A Master unto himself.

This is a fallacy because Man did not create Himself. God created him.

This 'spirit' has crept into the Body and we can see some of its manifestations such as rebellion to spiritual Authority, 'breakaway' Churches and Ministries.

An 'independent' spirit is a form of self will.

Forming your a Ministry and becoming the general Overseer is not success.

If God has not called one to such a position/responsibilities; this will simply be a display of an independent spirit/ individual ambition.

After all Joseph at the height of his leadership career was still reporting to Pharaoh.

Thou shalt be over my house, according unto thy word shall all my people be ruled: only in the throne will I be greater than thou - Genesis 41:40.

Daniel, in spite of his wisdom and greatness, still reported at various times to heathen kings.

At the end of the age, Jesus, the King of Kings will still be subject to God, his Father, our father.

Then cometh the end, when he shall have delivered up the kingdom to God, even the father; when he shall have put down all rule and all authority and power.

For he must reign, till he hath put all enemies under his feet.
The last enemy that shall be destroyed is death.
For he hath put all things under his feet. But when he saith all things are put under him, it is manifest that he is accepted, which put all things under him.
And when all things shall be subdued unto him, then shall the Son also himself be subject unto him that put all things under him that God may be all in all - I Corinthians 15: 24-28.

God, here in verse 28 refers to the Father.

At the new birth, the human spirit receives the Zoe life of God, 'comes alive' and thus becomes recreated. Thus Man is reconnected, reconciled, restored back into fellowship to God who sustains him through His Holy Spirit.

Man cannot, but be dependent on God, his source - The word of God.

And he answered and said, it is written, Man shall not live by bread alone, but by every word that proceedeth (present continuous) out of the mouth of God -Matthew 4:4

Man's nature desires to be his own master but the reality is that true liberty only comes from our dependence on God.

I am the vine, ye are the branches: He that abideth in me, and I in him, the same bringeth forth much fruit: for without me ye can do nothing -John 15: 5.

As the branches depend solely on the vine for nourishment; our only guarantee for sustainability and productivity also resides in staying 'positioned' in Christ. This is our primary and personal responsibility.

Thus saith the LORD; cursed be the man that trusteth in man, and maketh flesh his arm, and whose heart departed from the LORD.
For he shall be like the heath in the desert, and shall not see when good cometh; but shall inhabit the parched places in the wilderness, in a salt land and not inhabited. Blessed is the man that trusteth in the LORD, and whose hope the lord is. For he shall be as a tree planted by

the waters, and that spreadeth out her roots by the river, and shall not see when heat cometh, but her leaf shall be green; and shall not be careful in the year of drought, neither shall cease from yielding fruit -Jeremiah 17: 5-8.

And Jacob was left alone; and there wrestled a man with him until the breaking of the day. And when he saw that he prevailed not against him, he touched the hollow of his thigh; and the hollow of Jacob's thigh was out of joint, as he wrestled with him. -Genesis 32:24,25

Notice, the man was the one who wrestled with Jacob, not the other way round. Jacob's strong and independent will had always been the obstacle to God's plan, moves to reach and bless him.

God 'breaks' us because He loves and wants to bless us.

And as he passed over Penuel the sun rose upon him, and he halted upon his thigh -Genesis 32:31

Here we see Jacob 'limping'away after his encounter with God. When we encounter God, we can't hurry through life again. We see our own human limitations and understand the patience vital role in our walk of faith with God.

By faith Jacob, when he was dying, blessed both the sons of Joseph; and worshipped, leaning upon the top of his staff -Hebrews 11:21

After that encounter at Penuel, Jacob, for the remaining part of his life, used a staff to support himself. For him to worship God, he did not rely on his 'legs' - human strength or 'abilities'.

His leaning on his staff is symbolic in that he now relied on God for direction and more importantly had learnt that "the arm of flesh shall surely fail ".

One of the results of a having a divine experience with God is brokenness.

However, we do not need to have an 'encounter' (like in Jacob's case) with God, before we can have a 'broken spirit'.

We can become dependent on God by choice: obedience and cultivating submissive attitude to the Father's will.

For all those things hath mine hand made, and all those things have been, saith the LORD: but to this man will I look, even to him that is poor and of a contrite spirit, and trembleth at my word -Isaiah 66:2 See also Isaiah 57:15.

A man with a 'broken spirit' not only depends on God but also allows Him to set the pace for his life.

"Enoch walked with God but it was God that chose the directions and set the pace."

"The greatest warfare, we will ever face, is not with the devil or the world but against our flesh".

"A ruler indeed is one who has gained dominion over his flesh".

Chapter 2

Understanding His Body

And whether one member suffer, all the members suffer with it; or one member be honored, all the members rejoice with it
-I Corinthians 12: 12 -31.

Our scripture passage is from *I Corinthians 12: 12 -31.*

According to *1 John 4:16*, God is love. One of the attributes of love is sharing. That's one of the reasons why God chose and empowered man in *Genesis 1:26-30*, to share His eternal dominion by exercising authority on His behalf on the earth.

Now, we, the Church (His people whom He dwells in and with) are God's vessel of dominion on the earth and manifold wisdom.

To the intent that now unto the principalities and powers in the heavenly places might be known by the church the manifold wisdom of God -Ephesians 3:10.

God's greatest investment on the earth is not in things but His Body, the Church - God's embassy on the earth.

That's why we need to "know what is the hope of his calling, and what the riches of the glory of his inheritance (investment) in the saints" -Ephesians 1:18.

We can only function 'maximally' (reach our fullest potential) if we are planted in a Church/local body. That's the reason why we should understand His Body, its purpose and role in God's program on the earth.

Those that be planted in the house of the LORD shall flourish in the courts of our God. They shall still bring forth fruit in old age; they shall be fat and flourishing; to shew that the LORD is upright: he is my rock, and there is no unrighteousness in him -Psalm 92:13-15.

Every Minister or Ministry carries a unique grace or 'Spirit'
This is the dimension or portion of Christ that the Minister or Ministry is supposed to function in or supply to the body of Christ.

It's not for lordship but for service in God's Kingdom, serving God's preordained purposes in the lives of others.

Our greatest asset as the Body of Christ lies in our unity. Unity is not uniformity. It's more than saying or doing the same things.

It is a state of oneness that has to do with harmony in thought and purpose. In other words, we are brethren even though we may not belong to the same denomination, Movement, church or ministry.

Endeavoring to keep the unity of the Spirit in the bond of peace. There is one body, and one Spirit, even as ye are called in one hope of your calling; One Lord, one faith, one baptism. One God and Father of all, who is above all, and through all, and in you all -Ephesians4: 3-7.

God has not only put inside us different giftings and abilities but also places us in different positions in various Ministries, Churches which represent His Body here on earth; in line with his divine plan and purposes.

But unto every one of us is given grace according to the measure of the gift of Christ -Ephesians 4:7.

The reason why we have Denominations, Movements, Church or Ministries is for Operational purposes so that, as new creatures in God's Kingdom, we can fulfill God's call, to serve Him in varying capacities and places.

And now I am no more in the world, but these are in the world, and I come to thee. Holy Father, keep through thine own name those whom thou hast given me, that they may be one, as we are -John 17:11.

Neither pray I for these alone, but for them also which shall believe on me through their word: That they all may be one; as thou, Father, art in me, and I in thee, that they also may be one in us: that the world may believe that thou hast sent me.
And the glory which thou gavest me I have given them; that they may be one, even as we are one: I in them, and thou in me, that they may be made perfect in one; and that the world may know that thou hast sent me, and hast loved them, as thou hast loved me -John 17:21-23.

One of the reasons why the 'early' Church was successful was because of their unity: they moved together in the vehicle of "One Accord".

These all continued with one accord in prayer and supplication, with the women, and Mary the mother of Jesus, and with his brethren -Acts 1:14

And when the day of Pentecost was fully come, they were all with one accord in one place -Acts 2:1.

And the people with one accord gave heed unto those things which Philip spake, hearing and seeing the miracles, which he did -Acts 8:6.

How was this level of unity possible? It was because they obeyed the new commandment that the Lord gave his disciples in the Book of John.

A new commandment, I give unto you, that ye love one another; as I have loved you, that ye also love one another. By this shall all; men know that ye are my disciples, if ye have love one to another -John 13:34,35.

"Our strength, as Christ's Body does not lie in our various/unique giftings and diverse abilities but in our Oneness, unity and harmony."

Fulfill ye my joy, that ye be likeminded, having the same love, being of one accord, of one mind -Philippians 2:2

God' blessings, divine presence or anointing can be found in our unity.

Behold, how good and how pleasant it is for brethren to dwell together in unity! It is like the precious ointment upon the head that ran down upon the beard even Aaron's beard: that went down to the skirts of his garments; As the dew of Hermon and as the dew that descended upon the mountains of Zion: for there the LORD commanded the blessing, even life forever more -Psalm 133:1-3.

We have all drunk into the same Spirit, whether you are a Catholic, Anglican, protestant, Evangelical etc as long as we have genuinely accepted the Jesus Christ as our Lord and savior.

For by one Spirit are we all baptized into one body, whether we be Jews or Gentiles, whether we be Jews or Gentiles, whether we be bond or free: and have been all made to drink into one Spirit -I Corinthians 12:13.

Many Ministers or Ministries have' died' prematurely because they did not discern the Lord's body - walk in love.

For he that eateth and drinketh unworthily, eateth and drinketh damnation to himself, not discerning the Lord's body, For this cause many are weak and sickly among you, and many sleep. -I Corinthians 11:29,30.

What a tragedy, when we Christians don't live as we all belong to the same Body.

I am not referring to an 'ecumenical movement or universal Church system' or Church structure that is organized or based on a religious format, worldly system - 'spirit' of the world.

"One of the ways in which we can measure the strength of an army is to observe how it takes care of its casualties/injured".

We then that are strong ought to the infirmities of the weak, and not to please ourselves -Roman 15:1.

... and when thou art converted strengthen thy brethren -Luke 22:32.

How do we treat or care for the weak and fallen among us?

Him that is weak in the faith receive ye, but not to doubtful disputations (without passing judgment on disputable matters) -Romans 14: 1.

Whenever we criticize, cut down or condemn each other, we are either displaying our spiritual immaturity or have indirectly become Co-laborers with the devil:

(a) Displaying our spiritual immaturity: a judgmental and critical mindset/attitude is a manifestation of the carnal nature.

We don't have the right to judge someone else's servants, not to talk more or less of God's servant; even if he is the one God has set over you.

This is because every servant is accountable to his master or the One who has sent him.

Judge not, that ye be not judged. For with what judgment ye judge, ye shall be judged: and with what measure ye mete, it shall be measured to you again. -Mathew 7:1,2.

(b) Co laborers with the devil: the devil's ministry is to steal, and to kill and to destroy -John 10:10.

Just as God uses man to achieve His purposes on the earth, so the enemy seeks out men, even fellow Christians to achieve his purposes.

Harming each other through 'friendly fire' is not God's will.

We should help one another rather than pull others down, as is the way of the world

Bigger Ministries/Ministers (after all, they too started small) ought to encourage, inspire and support smaller ones, while smaller Ministries/ Ministers have the opportunity to learn from the 'senior' Ones.

The Church is the place for true deliverance and holiness.

But upon mount Zion shall be deliverance, and there shall be holiness, and the house of Jacob shall possess their possessions -Obadiah 1:17.

Divine Order

Divine Order plays a key role if we are to exercise spiritual authority in the Body of Christ.

Thus, in His infinite and divine wisdom, He has set the five-fold Ministry, in the Church to serve as 'under shepherds' under Jesus the great and good Shepherd.

A Call into Ministry should not be based on our Giftings, Manifestations of the Spirit, Prophetic word but on an active 'obedient' relationship with God as revealed (revelation knowledge) by His Holy Spirit.

The gifts and calling of God are without repentance -Romans 11:29.

... for many be called, but few chosen (qualify, pay the 'price' which makes them eligible to be selected) -Matthew 20:16.

Our work in the kingdom, when its according to "the script' already written by God for us to fulfill, not only counts for now but for eternity.

Thus, God gives us gifts and graces us with different capacities according to his preplanned purpose.

... But every man hath his proper gift of God, one after this manner, and another after that -I Corinthians 7:7.

That does not mean that we cannot develop our capacities and improve on our giftings. In fact we do these through our Obedience, sacrifice, practice and spiritual exercise.

Here we are referring to God's set role for our lives in the Body of Christ according to God's master plan.

It is possible to leave or derail from one's duty post.

Those who have, may still 'function', according their own understanding or people's perception, opinion or standards,

However in the Master's sight, Heaven's records, they are causing division, disaffection, schism and disunity in His Body.

Understanding God's preordained purpose for our lives will enable us to know what gift, ability to ask, desire from Him.

... and desire spiritual gifts... - I Corinthians 14:1.

Otherwise, our desires, requests may just be out of covetousness, our carnality/flesh, ignorance, worldly desires for Recognition, fame and to 'exercise' spiritual authority (not on God's terms nor for His purpose).

Ye ask, and receive not, because ye ask amiss, that ye may consume it on your lusts -James 4:3.

Because of the misunderstandings of these truths, many have not been able to function properly in the local Church or fulfill their God given destinies.

God connection: Relationship

While Spiritual authority positions us for exercising Godly authority, our connection with God is what actually determines the outcome of our venture of faith.

While David was under the authority of 'fallen' king Saul (not just on his own authority) for him to fight Goliath, we can clearly see that his victory over the philistine giant was as a result of his God connection: relationship.

Moses wasn't a great prophet, just because he was the leader of Israel but because he had a unique and intimate relationship with God: a key factor.

And he said, hear now my words; if there be a prophet among you, I the LORD will make myself known unto him in a vision, and will speak unto him in a dream. My servant Moses is not so, who is faithful in all mine house. With him will I speak mouth to mouth, even apparently, and not in dark speeches; and the similitude of the LORRD shall he behold; wherefore then were ye not afraid to speak against my servant Moses. -Numbers 12:6-8.

True/'Informed' followership

The goal of true followership should be discipleship.

Discipleship, is the process, through a conscious subjection to the discipline of the faith, that the nature and character of Christ is formed in the believer's life,

God wants us to be informed rather than dogmatic believers.
True follower ship has to do with our enthusiasm, attitude, diligence, desire for truth.

We see this trait exemplified by the Berean Christians, who earned Apostle Paul's commendation as being honorable.

These were more noble than those in Thessalonica, in that they received the word with all readiness of mind, and searched the scriptures daily whether those things were so -Acts 17:11.

Why? Because they sought confirmation of the teachings they were exposed to, not from others or themselves, or experiences but from the very word of God itself.

That's the reason why God has given us the 'anointing within'. It's our guarantee against deception.

These things have I written unto you concerning them that seduce you. But the anointing which ye have received of him abideth in you, and ye need not that any man teach you: but as the same anointing teacheth you all things, and is truth, and is no lie, even as it hath taught you, ye shall abide in him. - I John 2: 26,27.

There is no deception the presence of God.

For the word of God is quick, and powerful, and sharper than any two edged sword, piercing even to the dividing asunder of the soul and the spirit, and of the joints and marrow, and is a discerner of the thoughts and intents of the heart. Neither is there any creature that is not manifest in his sight: but all things are naked and opened unto the eyes of him with whom we have to do. -Hebrews 4:12,13.

The opposite of informed follower ship is ignorant, misinformed, 'religious', deceived or deformed follower ship. The children of Israel that died in the wilderness in the time of Moses fall in this category.

Such follower ship exerts a negative pull on leadership (as seen in the case of Moses) rather than enhance the leader's vision.

Ignorant followership, in a lot of cases, arises from a rejection of truth, rather than just an absence of knowledge.

My people are destroyed for lack of knowledge: because thou hast rejected knowledge, I will also reject thee, that thou shall be no priest to me: seeing thou hast forgotten the law of thy God, I will also forget thy children -Hosea 4: 6.

The Family Ministry

For this cause I bow my knees unto the Father of our Lord Jesus Christ, Of whom the whole family in heaven and earth is named -Ephesians3: 14, 15.

God is the head of the family in heaven (the saints, who having overcome, have slept in the Lord, and are now in heaven,) and earth (we, the body of Christ, who are still here on earth, whose duty now is to continue the family Ministry).

For through him we both have access by one Spirit unto the Father. Now therefore ye are no more strangers and foreigners, but fellow citizens with the saints, and of the household of God -Ephesians 2: 18, 19.

No wonder the scripture says that "God setteth the solitary (those living alone, without companions) in families; he bringeth out those which are bound with chains: but the rebellious dwell in a dry land -Psalm 68:6.

Jesus, the Son of God, our senior Brother, Captain of our salvation and our Commander in chief; having finished his earthly course, has instructed us to :

Go ye therefore, and teach all nations, baptizing them in the name of the Father, and the Son, and the Holy Ghost; Teaching them to observe all the things whatsoever I have commanded you: and lo, I am with you always, even unto the end of the world. Amen. -Matthew 28: 19, 20.

And he said unto them, how is it that ye sought me? Wist ye not that I must be about my father's business? -Luke 2: 49.

Christian Ministry is a spiritual business, run by God's family on biblical and not business principles obtainable in the world. Faith is the currency for transacting spiritual business.

It works by divine insight and obedience to the leadings, direction, and instruction of the Holy Ghost.

Positions, assignments and rewards are not allocated/ based on favoritism but rather on God's direction, training, Capacities and loyalty to the set man and his God given vision.

As a 'family business', every member, should become a disciple, who has not only drunk into the in the spirit of the 'house' but is committed to the vision of the set man or 'House'.

While Family member ship is based on our being born again, discipleship is all about commitment, responsibility and is premised on our 'continued exercise of faith' in God's word.

Then said Jesus to those Jews, which believed, on him, if ye continue in my word, then are ye my disciples indeed John 8:31.

The family Ministry is the greatest 'spiritual' business investment on the earth. It has no boundaries, be it racial, geographical, tribal, social, gender or otherwise.

For ye are all the children of God by faith in Christ Jesus. For as many of you as have been baptized into Christ have put on Christ. There is neither Jew nor Greek, there is neither bond nor free, there is neither male nor female: for ye are all one in Christ Jesus. And if ye be Christ's, then are ye Abraham's seed, and heirs according to the promise -Galatians 3:26-29.

In addition, God expects us to also transmit our legacy of serving Jesus, to our natural offspring.

... but as for me and my house, we will serve the LORD -Joshua 24:15.

In fact God is delighted, if this is so.

I know him, that he will command his children and his household after him, and they shall keep the way of the LORD, to do justice and judgment; that the LORD may bring upon Abraham that which he hath spoken of him -Genesis 18:19.

And if children, then heirs: heirs of God, and joint - heirs with Christ; if so be that we suffer with him, that we may be also glorified together -Romans 8:17.

Being born again automatically entitles the believer to be an heir to "the inheritance".

However, 'suffering with him' qualifies us to be joint- heirs (key shareholder or stake holders in the ultimate inheritance, which is to be glorified together) with Christ.

Surely His Body is the greatest family on the earth.

Chapter 3

The Set Man - a servant leader

And Moses spake unto the LORD, saying, Let the LORD, the God of the spirits of all flesh, set a man over the congregation, Which may go out before them, and which may go in before them, and which may lead them out, and which may bring them in; that the congregation of he LORD be not as sheep, which have no shepherd. -Numbers 27: 15 -17.

From the preceding verses in this passage, we see God making it known to Moses that he will not be allowed to lead the children of Israel into the Promised Land.

Moses, having realized this, asks (because of his passion for Israel and his assignment) God to select a successor.

In Christian Ministry, God's plan is not to build congregation, programs and structures but to build 'a man': lives, people.

Many may miss this point. What God does is to build 'a man', men who are carriers of God's glory or presence. Out of whose belly, rivers of living water will flow and produce these things: Buildings, programs, structures, etc.

In the last day, that great day of the feast, Jesus stood and cried, saying, if any man thirst, let him come unto me, and drink.
He that believeth on me, as the scripture hath said, out of his belly shall flow rivers of living water -John 7:37,38.

We see this pattern in the earthly ministry of our Lord Jesus Christ who had a mega ministry without formal Church buildings or walls.

For all those things hath mine hand made, and all those things have been, saith the LORD: but to this man will I look, even to him that is poor and of a contrite (repentant) spirit, and trembleth at my word -Isaiah 66:2.

The set man is an embodiment of God's representative grace. Every believer should be able to minister, but not every believer is called to be a Minister.

This 'man'is not set over buildings, programs, structures but people: God's people. Buildings, programs, structures etc are only instruments to assist the set man in achieving God's purposes concerning God's people.

As Christians, the concept of leadership is not about position or showmanship, but about stewardship, serving people, God's people.

Everyone is a leader in God's eyes because God has placed every believer in a position of influence or role in His Body for specific assignments.

The set man ought to be the servant leader because the ultimate display of Christian leadership is servant-hood.

Jesus knowing that the father had given all things into his hands, and that he was come from God, and went to God; He riseth from supper, and laid aside his garments; and took a towel and girded himself.
After that he poureth water into a bason, and began to wash the disciples' feet, and to wipe them with the towel wherewith he was girded. Then cometh he to Simon Peter; and Peter saith unto him, Lord, dost thou wash my feet? Jesus answered and said unto him, what I do thou knowest not now; but thou shalt know hereafter. Peter saith unto him, Thou shalt never wash my feet. Jesus answered him, if I wash thee not; thou hast no part with me. Simon Peter saith unto him, Lord, not my feet only, but also my hands and my head.
Jesus saith to him, He that is washed needeth not save to wash his feet, but is clean every whit: and ye are clean, but not all.

For he knew who should betray him; therefore said he, ye are not all clean. So after he had wad their feet, and had taken his garments, and was set down again, he said unto them, Know ye what I have done to you? Ye call me Master and Lord: and ye say well; for so I am.
If I then, your Lord and Master, have washed your feet; ye also ought to wash one another's feet. For I have given you an example that ye should do as I have done to you.
Verily, verily, I say unto you, the servant is not greater than his lord, neither he that is sent greater that he that sent him. If ye know these things, happy are ye if ye do them -John 13:3 -17.

What are these things? These things simply mean humbly serving God's purposes in the lives of others, which is one of the ways we can demonstrate our love for Jesus.

... lovest thou me more than these? ...Feed my lambs or sheep
-John 21:15 -17.

Feed the flock of God, which is among you, taking the oversight thereof, not by constraint, but willingly; not for filthy lucre, but of a ready mind;
Neither as being lords over God's heritage, but being ensamples to the flock
And when the chief Shepherd shall appear, ye shall receive a crown o glory that fadeth not away -I Peter 5:2-4.

Leadership by example is the hallmark of true Christian Ministry/leadership.

The credibility of the leader plays a crucial role in the area of follower ship.

And ye became followers of us, and of the Lord, having received the word in much affliction, with joy of the Holy Ghost- I Thessalonians 1: 4.

But Jesus answered them, My father worketh hitherto and I work
-John 5:17.

The state of our heart - motives, attitudes and desires determines or plays a vital role in the quality of our work.

It will also involve our faithfulness, diligence in labor or work.

We should ask ourselves questions such as, are we in the King's service for ourselves or for others? Is our motive borne out of a spirit of obedience, out of God's love and faith in our heart or not?

This is the heart connection - the key to success and excellence in Ministry.

Who is the Greatest?

And he came to Capernaum; and being in the house he asked them, what was it that ye disputed among yourselves by the way? But they held their peace: for by the way they had disputed among themselves, who should be the greatest. And he sat down, and called the twelve, and saith unto them, if any man desires to be the first, the same shall be the last of all, and servant of all. And he took a child, and set him in the midst of them; and when he had taken him in his arms, he said unto them. Whosoever shall receive one of such children in my name, receiveth me: and whosoever shall receive me, receiveth not me, but him that sent me. -Mark 9:33-37.

Neither be ye called master; for one is your Master, even Christ. But he that is greatest among you shall be your servant -Mathew 23: 10, 11.

God put inside all men the desire to create, do something of value worthy of being recognized, commended and rewarded.

To ignore this truth is simply to live in self denial; or being outright 'religious'.

However, we can express this innate desire by serving one another instead of lording it over others: which is the way of the world.

The Questions we should, however ask ourselves are:

(a) What are we supposed to create, do: our Assignment and

(b) Whose recognition, approval and reward should we seek?

He that speaketh of himself seeketh his own glory: but he that seeketh his glory that sent him, the same is true, and no unrighteousness is in him -John 7:18.

Passion /Hunger

Blessed are they who hunger and thirst after righteousness: for they shall be filled -Matthew 5:6.

Passion is the crucible where vision is birthed .The vision for the redemption of Man from sin was born out of God's passion for Man.

Passion is strong feeling, desire or liking while Compassion is the spiritual force/catalyst that releases God's divine or supernatural intervention on the earth to produce the miraculous (i.e. healing, salvation, deliverance etc).

For God so loved the world that he gave his only begotten Son, that whosoever believeth in him should not perish, but have everlasting life -John 3:16.

Passion is also not only visible but contagious. Our Passion for God is commensurate with the momentum of our pursuit to know Him.

We can lose our passion for God if we fill up or substitute our desire for Him with other 'things'.

As the hart panteth after the water brooks, so panteth my soul after thee, O God. -Psalm 42:1.

As many as I love, I rebuke and chasten: be zealous therefore, and repent -Revelations 3:19.

For the zeal of thine house hath eaten me up; and the reproaches of them that reproached thee are fallen upon me -Psalm 69: 9 John 2:17.

Spiritual fatherhood

For though ye have ten thousand instructors in Christ, yet have ye not many fathers; for in Christ Jesus I have begotten you through the gospel
Wherefore I beseech you, be ye followers of me -I Corinthians 4: 15,16.

Spiritual fathering is not about God fatherism or Mother hen syndrome, which operates in the world.

Your spiritual father is not automatically the person who 'led' you to Christ. Neither does it necessarily have to be your Pastor.

'Positional', the Pastor in a local Body is a spiritual father but playing that fathering role in your life will require his/her understanding of the dynamics of discipleship, Christian growth/maturity and mentorship. Otherwise, he may at best be an instructor to his congregation.

Spiritual fathering has to do with the One, who by God's grace, plays a crucial role in the developmental process of bringing another believer to a place of maturity and establishment in the faith, thus enabling the 'son' to fulfill God's s purpose in his or her life.

Spiritual fathering requires sacrifice, travail in prayer, patience, diligence and faith. We can see the example of Jesus Christ fathering the twelve disciples who later became apostles (excluding Judas Iscariot).

Focus

Looking unto Jesus the author and finisher of our faith; who for the joy set before him endured the cross, despising the shame, and is set down at the right hand of the throne of God -Hebrews 12:2

The 'eye' or our ability to visualize in our mind, imagination; plays a key role in the 'pursuit' of whatsoever we desire in life. It is a major gateway to the supernatural.

Usually, what we focus on or give our attention to determines to a large extent, our sense of value.

The light of the body is the eye; if therefore thine eye is single, thy whole body shall be full of light. But if thine eye be evil, thy whole body shall be full of darkness. If therefore the light that is in thee be darkness, how great is the darkness. -Matthew 6: 22, 23.

Look unto Abraham your father, and unto Sarah that bare you: for I called him alone, and blessed him, and increased him -Isaiah 51:2.

Without focus, we cannot get a sense of direction, which is needed to build and strengthen our faith.

Hell and destruction are never full; so the eyes of man are never satisfied -Proverbs 27:20.

Wisdom key: Don't let your heart always follow the desire of your eyes because your attention ultimately follows what you focus on.

Inner Caucus

And after six days Jesus taketh Peter, James and John his brother, and bringeth them up into an high mountain apart. And was transfigured before them: and his face did shine as the sun, and his raiment was white as the light -Matthew 17:1, 2.

And as they came down from the mountain, Jesus charged them saying, Tell the vision to no man, until the Son of Man be risen again from the dead -Matthew 17:9.

Jesus did not confide some things to all his disciples. It was not because he didn't love the others, but because, he knew those who had the capacity to be trusted with such information at that time.

Our state of devotion to the faith or level of maturity determines the level of revelation we can handle.

One of the hallmarks of great leadership is to know who to confide in and when to do so.

Called of God an high priest after the order of Melchisedec. Of whom we have many things to say and hard to be uttered, seeing ye are dull of hearing. For when for the time ye ought to be teachers, ye have need that one teach you again which be the first principles of the oracles of God; and are become such as have need of milk, and not of strong meat.
For every one that useth milk is unskillful in the word of righteousness: for he is a babe. But strong meat belongeth to them that are of full age, even those who by reason of use have their senses exercised to discern both good and evil -Hebrews 5:10 -14.

God is constrained by His love towards us not to reveal all things to us at once. Divine revelation is progressive, as we grow and mature in our walk with God.

Thus, we have the opportunity to develop our spiritual muscles and capacities to meet varying challenges as it comes.

Accountability
One of the components of stewardship is accountability.

The servant leader owes his primary accountability to God, the one who has called him.

Who art thou that judgest another man's servant? to his own master he standeth or falleth. Yea, he shall be holden up; for God is able to make him stand -Romans 14:4.

And the lord said, who then is that faithful and wise steward, whom his lord shall make ruler over his household, to give them their portion of meat in due season. Blessed is that servant whom his lord when he cometh shall find so doing -Luke 12:42,43.

However, God ordained leadership does not absolve the leader from the responsibility of providing feedback to his/her followers.

And being let go, they went to their own company, and reported all that the chief priests and elders had said unto them -Acts 4:23.

Here we see Peter and John (chief among the apostles) after been interrogated by the rulers, elders scribes and high priest of Israel, giving feedback to their company, body of believers that are committed to their doctrine.

Such action binds the team together and results in more commitment to the group cause.

Also, the servant leader needs to submit and be accountable to the Spiritual Authority God has directed him to.

Then fourteen years after I went up again to Jerusalem with Barnabas, and took Titus with me also. And I went up to by revelation, and communicated unto them that gospel which I preach among the Gentiles, but privately to them which were of reputation, lest by any means I should run, or had run, in vain. -Galatians 2: 1,2.

There may be a time when we need to crosscheck, verify of confirm our doctrine, with other Ministers or believers, who have already gone ahead of us. There is wisdom in this.

Delegation

And it came to pass on the morrow that Moses sat to judge the people; and the people stood by Moses from the morning unto the evening. And when Moses' father in law saw all that he did to the people, he said, what is this thing that thou doest to the people? Why sittest thou thyself alone, and all the people stand by thee from morning unto even?
And Moses said unto his father in law, because the people come unto me to inquire of God; When they have a matter, they come unto me: and I judge between one and another, and I do make them know the statutes of God, and his laws.
And Moses father in law said unto him. the thing that thou doeth is not good. Thou wilt surely wear away, both thou, and this people that

is with thee: for this thing is too heavy for thee; thou art not able to perform it thyself alone.
Hearken now unto my voice, I will give thee counsel, and God shall be with thee: Be thou for the people to God-ward, that thou mayest bring the causes unto God.
And thou shalt teach them ordinances and laws, and shalt shew them the way wherein they must walk, and the work that they must do.
Moreover thou shalt provide out of all the people able men, such as fear God, men of truth, hating covetousness; and place such over them, to be rules of thousands, and rulers of hundreds, rulers of fifties, and rulers of tens.
And let them judge the people at all seasons: and it shall be, that every great matter they shall bring unto thee, but every small matter they shall judge: so shall it be easier for the thyself, and they shall bear the burden with thee.
If thou shalt do this thing, and God command thee so, then thou shalt be able to endure, and all this people shall also go to their place in peace. So Moses hearkened to the voice of his father in law, and did all that he had said.
And Moses chose able men out of all Israel, and made them heads over the people, rulers of thousands, rulers of hundreds, rulers of fifties, and rulers of tens.
And they judged the people at all seasons: the hard causes they brought unto Moses, but every small matter they judges themselves -Exodus 18: 13-26.

From the above, we can clearly see that Delegation is an antidote to spiritual, mental and physical 'burnout' and ineffectiveness.

We see a similar scenario in the appointment of the Deacons in the early Church in Acts 6:1-7.

But we will give ourselves continually to prayer, and to the ministry of the word. -Acts 6:4.

The result of this wise decision can be seen later on in increased productivity and efficiency.

And the word of God increased; and the number of the disciples multiplied in Jerusalem greatly; and a great company of the priests were obedient to the faith -Acts 6:7.

We can also see from the above, that delegation enables us to prioritize, so that we can concentrate on handling core and more relevant issues.

Succession

Obviously, the ministry of the set man is not complete without a successor succession Plan.

The principle of succession planning emanated from God Himself.

God, who at sundry times and in divers manners spake in time past unto the fathers by the prophets, Hath in these last days spoken unto us by his Son, whom he hath appointed heir of all things, by whom also he made the worlds. -Hebrews 1: 1, 2.

One of the reasons why God made Jesus, the heir of all things was not only because he is the Son of God, but also because of Jesus' Commitment, competence, and proven obedience.

Though he were a Son, yet learned he obedience by the things which he suffered; And being made perfect, he became the author of eternal salvation unto all them that obey him. -Hebrews 5:8, 9.

Succession is a spiritual transaction, which should not be based on natural family ties or other fleshy, carnal considerations.

To do otherwise is to act 'politically', which is the way of the world.

Only spiritual sons are qualified to succeed the set man.

However, it does not mean that a spouse, his natural son/daughter or relative cannot succeed the leader, if there are spiritual 'sons'.

Succession is an important aspect in any ministry, as 'sons' are the only ones that carry the vision of the set man to the next level and continue with 'the work'.

Some Ministers have fallen into this trap of trying to 'personalize' the ministry God has given them by either selecting their spouse or any of their children as their successor.

This normally results in the 'wrong person' being placed in the right position.

Wrong in the sense that they may not be competent to handle the challenges that go along with such responsibilities.

Now the sons of Eli were sons of Belial; they knew not the LORD.
And the priest's custom with the people was, that when any man offered sacrifice, the priests' servant came, while the flesh was in seething, with a flesh hook of three teeth in his hand.
And he struck it into the pan, or kettle, or caldron, or pot; all that the flesh hook brought up the priest took for himself. So they did in Shiloh unto all the Israelites that came thither.
Also before they burnt the fat, the priest's servant came, and said to the man that sacrificed, Give flesh to roast for the priest: for he will not have sodden flesh of thee, but raw. And if any man said unto him, let them not fail to burn the fat presently, and then take as much as thy soul desireth; then he would answer him, nay; but thou shall give it me now: and if not will take it by force.
Wherefore the sin of the young men was very great before the LORD: for men abhorred the offering of the LORD -I Samuel 2: 12-17.

Samuel repeated a similar mistake in his old age and thus gave the elders of Israel an occasion or a reason (to 'hide' under, by asking for a king) to reject God.

And it came to pass, when Samuel was old, that he made his sons judges over Israel.
Now the name of his first born was Joel; and the name of his second, Abiah, they were judges in Beersheba.

And his sons walked not in his ways, but turned aside after lucre, and took bribes, and perverted judgment -I Samuel 8: 1-3.

Another pitfall of making a wrong choice in succession (after natural lines), is that it leads to a breakdown of discipline.

The set man, in such cases, places himself in a position where he lacks the will power to exercise his God given authority to discipline.

His self-imposed handicap, nonetheless cannot excuse him from his responsibility to God and the congregation/people God has given to, or placed him over.

We see this in the case of Eli and Samuel. There was no record that they ever disciplined their children or corrected the situation.

In Eli's case, (as we can see in *I Samuel 2:27-36*), it attracted God's judgment.

Leadership is not about position but purposeful living: serving God's purposes in other people's lives .It has to do with the state of our heart, attitude and perspective to life.

Then said Jesus to his disciples, if any man will come after me, let him, deny himself, and take up his cross, and follow me. For whosoever will save his life shall lose it; and whosoever will lose his life for my sake shall find it. For what is a man profited, if he shall gain the whole world, and lose his soul or what shall a man give in exchange for his soul?

For the Son of man shall come in the glory of his father with his angels; and then he shall reward every man according to his works -Matthew 16:24 -27.

In whatever position (Pastors, Husbands, wives, sons, Masters, servants etc); we find ourselves in life, we ought to be servant leaders.

Chapter 4

The Gifts of God

The purpose of God's gifts to His Body is to: minister to the LORD (worship, praise, thanksgiving, giving Him glory), minister to the Body of Christ (nurture, encourage, inspire) and minister to the World (witness, salvation, deliverance etc).

The Gifts of God: the Father

God, the Father of is the source and giver all good things.

From Him proceeded the Son (our lord and savior Jesus Christ) and the Spirit (the Holy Ghost).

Jesus said unto them. If God were your Father, ye would love me: for I proceeded forth and came from God; neither came I of myself, but he sent me -John 8:42.

But when the Comforter is come, whom I will send unto you from the Father, even the Spirit of truth, which proceedeth from the Father, he shall testify of me -John 15:26.

Every good and every perfect gift is from above, and cometh down from the Father of lights, with whom is no variableness, neither shadow of turning -James 1: 17.

In *Hebrews 6: 4*, Jesus is referred to as the heavenly gift.

We see the Father giving us Jesus, this heavenly gift, for our redemptive salvation.

For God so loved the world, that he gave his only begotten Son, that whosoever believeth in him should not perish, but have everlasting life -John 3:16.

The Holy Ghost is also referred to as the good gift that the Father gives to us, His children.

If ye then, being evil, know how to give good gifts unto your children: how much more shall your heavenly Father give the Holy Spirit to them that ask him? -Luke 11:13.

In *Acts 1: 13,14*, we see that this was exactly what Jesus disciples did in the Upper room that ushered in the coming of the Holy Ghost in his fullness unto planet earth as was experienced in Acts Chapter 2.

In *Acts 10:45*, the Holy Ghost is referred to as the gift that was poured out.

However, since that time till now, the Holy Ghost has been around and all we need to do if we desire a similar experience, like that of the day of Pentecost, is to receive Him into our lives by exercising our faith in the name of Jesus.

The Gifts of the Son

This mainly refers to what is known as the Five-fold Ministry.

But unto every one of us is given grace according to the measure of the gift of Christ. Wherefore, he saith, when he ascended up on high, he led captivity captive, and gave gifts unto men.
(Now that he ascended, what is it but that he also descended first into the lower parts of the earth? He that descended is the same also that ascended up far above all heavens, that he might fill all things).
And he gave some, apostles; and some prophets; and some, pastors and teachers;

For the perfecting of the saints, for the work of the ministry, for the edifying of the body of Christ:
Till we all come in the unity of the faith, and of the Son of God, unto a perfect man, unto the measure of the stature of the fullness of Christ -Ephesians 4:7-13.

The Gifts of the Holy Ghost
There are nine major gifts of the Holy Ghost.
We can classify them into three categories

(a) The Revelatory gifts (word of wisdom, knowledge and discerning of spirits),

(b) The Power gifts (faith, gifts of healing and working of miracles) and

(c) The Utterance gifts (prophecy, divers: kinds of tongues and interpretation of tongues).

Now there are diversities of gifts, but the same Spirit. And there are differences of administrations, but the same Lord. And there are diversities of operations, but it is the same God, which worketh all in all. But the manifestation of the Spirit is given to every man to profit withal. For to one is given by the Spirit, the word of wisdom; to another the word of knowledge by the same Spirit; To another faith by the same Spirit another the gifts of healing by the same Spirit; To another the working of miracles; to another prophecy; to another discerning of spirits; to another divers kinds of tongues; to another the interpretation of tongues But all these worketh that one and the selfsame Spirit, dividing to every man severally as he will.
-I Corinthians 12:4-11.

Other gifts of the Holy Ghost can be seen in Romans 12 and I Peter 4.

Having then gifts differing according to the grace that is given to us, whether prophecy, let us prophesy according to the proportion of faith; Or ministry let us with on our ministering (helps, music etc): or he that teacheth, on teaching (this is not the office of a teacher);

Or he that exhorteth, on exhortation (encourage, motivational abilities); he that giveth (helps, supportive gifs such as financiers to the gospel) let him do it in simplicity, he that ruleth (administration), with diligence ; he that sheweth mercy (compassion, 'humanitarian') with cheerfulness. -Romans 12: 6-8.

As every man hath received the gift, even so minister the same one to another, as good stewards of the manifold grace of God.
If any man speak, let him speak as the oracles of God; if any man minister, let him do it as of the ability which God giveth; that God in all things may be glorified through Jesus Christ, to whom be praise and dominion for ever and ever, Amen -I Peter 4:10,11.

The above list (gifts of the Holy Ghost) is not exhaustive.

And it shall come to pass afterward, that I will pour out my spirit upon all flesh; and your sons and your daughters shall prophesy, your old men shall dream dreams, your young men shall see visions:
And also upon the servants and upon the handmaids in those days will I pour out my spirit. -Joel 2:28,29; Acts 2: 17,18.

Being the Carrier and Distributor of God's gifts, the Holy Spirit also gives gifts such as interpretation of dreams, special skills and abilities.

The Anointing

How God anointed Jesus of Nazareth with the Holy Ghost and with power; who went about doing good and healing all that were oppressed of the devil; for God was with him. -Acts 10:38.

From the above, we see how Jesus (the last Adam) was anointed with the Holy Spirit so as to exercise dominion in a fallen world system; minister during his three and half years of ministry.

Jesus' lifestyle, during those years, show us how we, the new creation (Dominion Man) is supposed to live.

This glorious lifestyle - Anointed 'new creation man' living and ruling in an imperfect environment(planet earth), is the our heritage which we ought to manifest.

And John bare record, saying, I saw the Spirit descending from heaven like above, and it abode upon him -John 1:32.

In like manner we (his generation) need the anointing, as a restorative instrument, for ruling in a fallen world.

What is the anointing? The word anointing in its self, means to rub or smear on.

However, in our Christian context, it can be viewed as God immersing a believer or rubbing him/her all over in/with His Spirit.

Here, we are not referring to the anointing within (needed for spiritual growth, development and maturity) in a believer's life; as we see in I John 2:27.

Rather we are talking about the Operations of the Holy Ghost in a believer's life, empowering /enabling him to serve God's purposes on the earth. It's God's ability for exercising His dominion, through us, on the earth.

Every anointing is governmental in nature. This is because the anointing is the God's ability or spiritual instrument that enables a man to govern or rule over his God given sphere of influence, thereby, fulfilling God's mandate for his original creation - Man.

However, the dimensions and operations of governance may differ.

It takes the anointing to confront idolatry and religious spirits.

We cannot 'improve' on God's anointing.

I know that whatsoever, God doeth, it shall be forever: nothing can be put to it, nor any thing taken from it; and God doeth it, that men should fear before him -Ecclesiastes 3:14.

However, we can increase it, or in its operation, by as we submit to God's will through our lifestyle of Obedience and sacrifice.

Anointing, supernatural grace enables us to labour and work smart as we expand the frontiers of God's kingdom on the earth. This assignment requires our diligence.

While we need the anointing to activate our God given inherent potentials, Diligence is the key to developing such potentials.

We may not be able to fully fulfill our divine destiny, if we haven't developed our potentials or matured in the Faith.

'Anointed' without the Anointing

But the Spirit of the LORD departed from Saul, and an evil spirit from the LORD troubled him -I Samuel 16: 14.

The correct translation of the latter part of the above verse should have being in the permissive sense.

For we know that evil spirits don't come from God. If this were so, it will be contrary to the nature and character of God - a fact buttressed by understanding the totality of scriptures.

This then is the message which we have heard of him and declare unto you, that God is light, and in him is no darkness at all -I John 1: 5.

Therefore hearken unto me ye men of understanding: far be it from God, that he should do wickedness; and from the Almighty, that he should commit iniquity. For the work of a man shall he render unto him, and cause every man to find according to his ways. Yea, surely God will not do wickedly, neither will the Almighty pervert judgment -Job 34: 10-12.

Obviously, the spirit of God via the anointing was a 'covering' for Saul from the activity of demonic forces.

Once the Holy Ghost departed, he became vulnerable to the influence of such forces - he became like an ordinary man. No wonder he could not lead Israel to battle against the philistine giant Goliath in I Samuel 17.

Failed leadership cannot confront the Goliaths.

And the Philistine said, I defy the armies of Israel this day; give me a man that we may fight together. When Saul and all Israel heard those words of the Philistine, they were dismayed, and greatly afraid
-I Samuel 17:10, 11.

And he said unto his men, The LORD forbid that I should do this thing unto my master, the LORD's anointed, to stretch forth mine hand against him, seeing he is the anointed of the LORD -I Samuel 24:6.

Behold, this day thine eyes have seen how that the lord had delivered thee to day into mine hand in the cave; and some bade me kill thee, but mine eye spared thee; and I said, I will not put forth mine hand against my lord; for he is the LORD's anointed -I Samuel 24:10.

We can see that David still saw Saul as God's anointed.

And David said to Abishai, Destroy him not, for who can stretch forth his hand against the LORD's anointed, and be guiltless? -I Samuel 26:9.

Who can speak ill of another brother/leader/fellow Minister in Christ, (especially in public or on the pulpit) and be guiltless or innocent?

Any believer that breaks this 'rule of engagement' will have to give an account to God for his/her action or indiscretion.

And David said furthermore, As the LORD liveth, the LORD shall smite him; or his day shall come to die; or he shall descend into battle, and perish. The LORD forbid that I should stretch forth mine hand against the LORD's anointed... -I Samuel 26:10,11.

It will be inappropriate for any one who tries to "remove" another minister, even if he perceives that such a servant of God has derailed from God.

"It's God's, not any man's, sole prerogative to judge his ministers ".

While we see the story of David, a shepherd boy becoming a giant Killer in Chapters 16 and 17 of I Samuel, what we see from Chapters 17 to 31 of I Samuel is the reign of Saul, a king without 'the anointing', struggling to keep his position, rather than seeking God's face for restoration.

Those who have lost God's Anointing struggle for positions. Not because they want to serve God's purposes in the lives of others but because they want others to serve them.

Instead of Saul mentoring David, he became an oppressor who saw David as a threat that should be eliminated.

Since, he no longer had access to divine strategies, which comes via the anointing; he had to resort to unscriptural means of leading God's people.

Here we see a "performer and not a proof producer".

A leader who no longer has or flows in God's anointing normally resorts to Gimmicks, manipulation, intimidation and all sorts of carnal devices to 'maintain' control and keep Himself in 'power'.

In *II Samuel 1: 17 - 27* we see David's lamentation over Saul and Jonathan his son.

Note Verse 21, Ye mountains of Gilboa, let there be no dew, neither let there be rain, upon you, nor fields of offering: for there the shield of the mighty is vilely cast away, the shield of Saul, as though he had not been anointed with oil.

Title chasing is a strong evidence of the absence of the anointing and the manifestation of the flesh.

Unhealthy/ strong desire for self-recognition/glorification is an attribute of haughtiness, pride and worldliness.

A man truly called of God doesn't need to acquire titles - His Eminence, Holiness, Archbishop, Superior, etc.

Any man who loses God's anointing and continues to minister/function without it is treading on dangerous grounds.

He may lose the position where God has placed him, and possibly ultimately, also ultimately lose his life; may not fulfill the number of his days on the earth - premature death.

Saul lost the anointing, (through disobedience to God's instructions), and later on, the throne and his life.

Many years down the line, we find King David committing adultery with Bathsheba (the wife of Uriah the Hittite) and murdering the husband.

We see David in deep repentance, crying to God for His mercy not to take the anointing from his Life.

Repentance in simple terms means to "to turn back or return to God".

Cast me not away from thy presence: and take not thy holy spirit from me. -Psalm 51:11.

Having seen, years earlier before, the fate that befell king Saul, he must have realized one thing: God's anointing over or on your life is what makes you relevant in His service/program and not your occupation of 'the throne'.

It's like a man going war (without ammunition) with an enemy (who has an inferior weapon), but knows that there is no ammunition.

Such a man can only shoot blank bullets - make noise without making the impact expected of him.

Having a form of godliness, but denying the power thereof, from such turn away -II Timothy 3:5.

... clouds they are without water... -Jude: 12.

In Chapters 15-18 of the book of II Samuel, when David later on, and due to God's judgment, lost the throne to his son Absalom (though temporarily), but not the anointing.

We can, just like David, cultivate a similar sense of great value (which influenced David's strong determination/disposition not to lose the anointing under any circumstance) for God's anointing.

Spiritual Maturity

Spiritual maturity is not synonymous with the Anointing or how many years we have been 'saved'.

A man can be heavily anointed or born again for many years and still not yet spiritually mature.

However, there is no way someone can be classified as being 'spiritually mature' without walking in God's anointing.

For when for the time ye ought to be teachers, ye have need that one teach you again which be the first principles of the oracles of God; and are become such as have need of milk, and not strong meat.
For every one that useth milk is unskillful in the word of righteousness, for he is a babe. But strong meat belongeth to them who are of full age, even those who by reason of use have their senses exercised to discern both good and evil -Hebrews 5:12-14.

At the new birth, we are all children of God.

The Spirit itself beareth witness with our spirit, that we are the children of God -Romans 8:16.

However, the purpose of our spiritual growth and developmental process is for us to be able to recognize, agree, yield and cooperate with the will of God for our lives.

This is a vital essence of the Christian faith.

For as many as are led by the Spirit of God, they are the sons of God -Romans 8:14.

In other words, being led by the Holy Ghost is the test for spiritual maturity.

Apostle Paul addressed the Corinthian Church as babes in spite of the fact that they were experiencing various manifestations of the Holy Ghost.

And I, brethren, could not speak unto you as unto spiritual, but as unto carnal, even as unto babes in Christ. -I Corinthians 3:1.

When I was a child, I spake as a child, I understood as a child, I thought as a child: but when I became a man, I put away childish things -I Corinthians 13:11.

"Our gifting promote, places us in a position to do, fulfill divine assignment while our character is developed in the process of fulfilling that assignment".

Transfer of gifts via Impartation
Our scripture passage reading is from II Kings 2:1-25.

God is in the business of continuity and increase.

That's the reason why, especially in the area of service, He can transfer the Operational dimensions 'auction' of the Holy Spirit from One believer into the life of another. This is always in accordance with His plan and purposes.

However, we need to exercise our faith through Spirit filled prayers, which gets heaven's attention, for us to receive such impartations or blessings.

And it came to pass, when they were gone over, that Elijah said unto Elisha , Ask what I shall do for thee, before I be taken away from thee, And Elisha said, I pray thee, let a double portion of thy spirit be upon me. And he said, Thou hast asked a hard thing nevertheless, if thou see me when I am taken from thee, it shall be so unto thee; but if not, it shall not be so. -II Kings 2:9,10.

One of the reasons why Elijah said that the request was 'a hard thing' was because Elisha had asked for a double portion - twice of God's manifest ability, power and presence in Operation in Elijah's life.

However, as we see later on in the story, God honored Elijah's faith just as Elisha fulfilled the Elijah's condition - saw Elijah taken to up by a whirlwind into heaven (II Kings 2:11,12).

This, process of 'transfer', which is called impartation, is about spiritual operations, giftings, abilities, etc, and not human spirits.

And when the sons of the prophets which were to view at Jericho saw him, they said, The spirit of Elijah doth rest on Elisha, And they came to meet him, and bowed themselves to the ground before him
-II Kings 2:15.

Note the words used "The spirit of Elijah doth rest on Elisha". This is referring to the unique anointing, (which was formerly in operation in Elijah's life and ministry) now transferred and resident on Elisha.

How did they know? Because, in the previous verse (14), they saw Elisha divide river Jordan, and recognized that such manifestation, could only have been possible if Elisha was carrying Elijah's anointing.

What they might not have known at that time, was that Elisha had been given a double portion of his master's anointing.

We can also transfer spiritual gifts through laying on of hands.

And Joshua the son of Nun was full of the spirit of wisdom; for Moses had laid his hands upon him: and the children of Israel hearkened unto him, and did as the LORD commanded Moses -Deuteronomy 34:8.

Wherefore I put thee in remembrance that thou stir up the gift of God, which is in thee by the putting on of my hands -II Timothy 1:6

From the above scripture, it is possible that Apostle Paul, (in reference to the word 'the gift of God"), was not only referring to the gift of salvation, but a specific impartation from the Holy Spirit.

This is scriptural and forms part of the foundational doctrines of the faith, the doctrine of baptisms, and of laying on of hands (not only for healing the sick)... -Hebrews 6:2.

God also imparts spiritual gifts, 'graces' and abilities to us as we fellowship with Him in His word, prayer, praise, worship etc.

God's design is for us to be the human vessels through which He can manifests his gifts.

From another perspective, that human vessel can be seen as a gift to others.

"Thus, today, YOU, the new creation in Christ, are God's gift to mankind and this generation".

Who is the new creation?

The new Creation

Therefore if any man be in Christ, he is a new creature: old things are passed away; behold all things are become new -II Corinthians 5:17.

This specie of being never existed before; Only Adam and Eve (before the Fall) can be comparable to him.

Man is the only specie that was made in the image and likeness of God.

And God said, let us make man in our image, after our likeness...
-Genesis 1:26.

Angels are not made in God's image or likeness, though they have God's glory upon them. The new creature is the only being now in creation that has the capacity to know God as Father.

Angels only know God as God, not as Father.

Jesus saith unto her, Touch me not; for I am not yet ascended to my Father; but go to my brethren, and say unto them, I ascend unto my Father, and your Father and to my God, and your God -John 20:17.

The new creature is greater than any Old Testament saint, be it Enoch, Abraham, Moses, Daniel, David, Elijah, John the Baptist, etc.

For I say unto you, among those that are born of women there is not a greater prophet than John the Baptist, but he that is least in the kingdom of God is greater than he -Luke 7:28.

Being born again, not of corruptible seed, but of incorruptible by the word of God, which liveth and abideth forever -I Peter 1:23

He is not (was) a sinner. Instead, he is a saint redeemed by the blood of Jesus.

Neither is he a product of sin but the product of God's righteousness, love, wisdom, power and glory.

Wherefore hence forth know we no man after the flesh: yea, though we have known Christ after the flesh, yet now henceforth know we him no more -II Corinthians 5:16

Just like we are supposed to know Christ after the Spirit, the new creature ought to be known and understood by the Spirit.

The wind bloweth where it listeth, and thou hearest the sound thereof, but canst not tell whence it cometh, and whither it goeth; so is every one that is born of the Spirit -John 3:8.

The new creature is born from above and thus has dual citizenship:

(a) A citizen of the earth by virtue of being a human being

(b) A citizen of heaven by virtue of being in Christ

They are the ones whom God has entrusted with the ministry of reconciliation.

And all things are of God, who hath reconciled us to himself by Jesus Christ, and hath given to us the ministry of reconciliation.
-II Corinthians 5:18.

For we are his workmanship, created in Christ Jesus unto good works, which God hath before ordained that we should walk in them.
-Ephesians 2:10.

His Occupation army, responsible for enforcing His will, judgments and purpose on the earth.

Thou art my battle axe and weapons of war, for with thee will I break in pieces the nations, and with thee will I destroy kingdoms -Jeremiah 51:20.

Now then we are ambassadors for Christ, as though God did beseech you by us: we pray you in Christ's stead, be ye reconciled to God.
-II Corinthians 5:20.

Ye are the salt of the earth... -Matthew 5:13.

Ye are the light of the world... -Matthew 5:14.

God has designed the new creature, by nature to carry His glory.

Let your light so shine before men, that they may see your good works, and glorify your Father which is in heaven -Matthew 5:16.

Chapter 5

Dominion -the spirit of service

And God said; Let us make man in our image, after our likeness and let them have dominion over the fish of the sea, and over the fowl of the air, and over the cattle, and over all the earth, and over every creeping thing that creepeth upon the earth. So God created man in his own image, in the image of God created he him; male and female created he them -Genesis 1:26, 27.

Here we see God's original mandate for Man on the earth.

We should note that "every creeping thing that creepeth upon the earth" includes Satan and all his evil associates.

By inference, we can deduce that from *Genesis 1:26, 27*, that Man (as a spirit being) was not kept in the dark that there an evil one (the devil existed), which he ought to subdue and dominate.

This was before man's (male and female) body was formed or he became a living soul and placed in the garden of Eden -Genesis 2:7, 8.

God did not place us on the earth to show us how big satan is but to exercise authority over the evil one and his agents.

And the LORD said unto satan, Whence comest thou? Then satan answered the LORD, and said, from going to and fro in the earth, and from walking up and down in it -Job1: 7.

That's how we know that satan is an unemployed (dismissed by God for treason) fallen angel, wandering all over or 'creeping' the earth just to do evil.

The whole world is under the control of the evil one, satan who is the god of this world.

And we know that we are of God, and the whole world lieth in wickedness -I John 5:19.

However, there are two kingdoms from which dominion can be exercised over the world: the kingdom of light: our lord and savior, Jesus Christ and satan's kingdom of darkness.

While both kingdoms are in the heavenlies, the kingdom of light is the superior, conquering, reigning, and eternally ruling kingdom.

This is where the' new creation' in Christ lives and exercises his authority (which is first spiritual in nature), dominion and ruler ship from.

For our conversation is in heaven: from whence also we look for the Saviour, the Lord Jesus Christ:
Who shall change our vile body, that it may be fashioned like unto his glorious body, according to the working whereby he is able even to subdue all things unto himself -Philippians 3:20.

This kingdom of dominion can be referred to as 'heaven' or the higher heavens.

Who hath delivered us from the power of darkness, and hath translated us into the kingdom of his dear Son -Colossians 1:13

"This is the good news, we have been redeemed from a lower kingdom; to and are now, rulers in the Higher One- the kingdom of light."

But ye are a chosen generation, a royal priesthood, an holy nation, a peculiar people; that ye should shew forth the praises of him who hath called you our of darkness into his marvelous light -I Peter 2:9.

However with the fall of Man, Dominion or ruler ship can now be exercised in two dimensions:

(a) Over our flesh, the world and the devil

(b) Serving God, and His purposes in the life of others.

But Jesus called them unto him, and said, Ye know that the princes of the Gentiles exercise dominion over them, and they that are great exercise authority upon them. But it shall not be so among you: but whosoever will be great among you let him be your minister;
And whosever will be chief among you, let him be your servant; Even as the Son of man came not to be ministered unto, but to give his life a ransom for many -Matthew 20: 25-28.

True Dominion is born out of Agape Love, which seeks out God's best for other person. Dominion not born out of love will only produce 'spiritual tyrants, bullies'.

These are those who use the occasion of their God given authority to gratify their fleshy cravings, carnal desire, exploiting their followers or those under their authority for personal gain.

Today, the Body of Christ, the Church (His people whom He dwells in and with) is God's dominion vessel for ruling the earth.

While we are supposed to serve humbly one another in love, we are however required to exercise dominion over all things, circumstances, events and demonic spirits (illegal agents on the earth).

Adam and Eve, his wife, before the fall, were perfect human beings living in perfect environment. They were not only surrounded by the glory of God but their entire being was permeated with that glory.

However, when they fell from glory, Man not only died (separated from communion with God) but also became sense ruled before physical death.

As for man, his days are as grass: as a flower of the field, so he flouriseth. For the wind passeth over it, and it is gone; and the place thereof shall know it no more -Psalm 104:15, 16

The voice said, Cry. And I said, what shall I cry? All flesh is grass, and all their goodliness (glory) is as the flowers of the field.
The grass withereth, and the flower faded because the spirit (breath) of the LORD bloweth upon it: surely the people is grass. The grass withereth and the flower faded: but the word of our God shall stand forever -Isaiah 40:6,7.

Man only comes 'alive' when He receives Jesus as His Lord and Savior.

For God so loved the world, that He gave His only begotten Son, that whosoever believeth in him should not perish, but have everlasting life -John 3: 16.

While 'natural' Man (with fallen nature) takes his identity from Adam or the earth; we, God's new creation in Christ Jesus, have our identity rooted in Christ, the Lord from heaven.

Our revelation of who we are in Christ is very important for us to serve Him or exercise dominion as He expects us to do.

Probation Period: a divine pattern

And the LORD God planted a garden eastward in Eden; and there he put the man whom he had formed -Genesis 2:8.
And the LORD God took the man, and put him into the garden of Eden to dress it and to keep it. -Genesis 2:15

Here, we see Adam placed on 'probation' in the garden of Eden.

What do we mean, in this context, by 'probation' ?

Probation period is a time of 'trial', assessment in which God examines, tests us before confirming, attesting, empowering and releasing us into His future purposes / higher responsibilities.

The LORD is in his holy temple, the LORD's throne is in heaven: his eyes behold, his eyelids try, the children of men
The LORD trieth the righteous.......... -Psalm 11:4,5.

It is a preparatory stage or 'training period' prior to God elevating us to the next level in our walk with Him and service in His kingdom.

It does not mean that we will no longer be tested or assessed after probation period but that we have moved to a 'significant' level in our relationship with God and service in his kingdom.

Adam's assignment was to dress (cultivate, improve the yield, maximize the potentials of the garden) and keep (protect, fence it from intruders - exercise ownership).

Why does God not give us finished products?

It's because He wants us to engage our creative potentials, abilities in the process of producing something from another thing.

This 'production process', which predates the 'fall', can be defined as work.

That's the reason why there were trees in the gardenof Eden, from which Adam and Eve could make chairs, tables. They could kill the animals to get food and clothing.

Nowadays, many are engaged with jobs, which have no bearing to the original purpose of God for their lives. Such have indirectly become slaves to the world 'Babylonian' system.

Also, the garden of Eden was supposed to be the center or model from where development, population and infrastructures will begin to spread to Eden and the whole earth.

Adam was created innocent and sinless, while Jesus was born innocent and sinless.

However, in spite of the fact that God put Adam in the garden of Eden (an atmosphere filled with God's presence: on a perfect earth) and gave him an helpmate; Adam still sinned

Thus he failed his 'probation' and therefore, could not fulfill God's original intention for Man in -Genesis 1:26.

Unlike Adam, Jesus (who lived in an imperfect environment: an earth that was already corrupted as a result of the fall of Adam and had no helpmate) never sinned.

Hereafter I will not talk much with you, for the prince of this world cometh, and hath nothing in me -John 14:30.

For we have an high priest which cannot be touched with the feeling of our infirmities: but was in all points tempted like as we are, yet without sin -Hebrews 4:15.

Though he were a Son, yet learned he obedience by the things, which he suffered; And being made perfect, he became the author of eternal salvation unto all them that obey him. -Hebrews 5: 8, 9.

Here, we see Jesus passing his 'probation' period, before he could be certified as the savior of Mankind.

Where the first Adam failed, Jesus (the last Adam) excelled and thus qualified to fulfill God's original intention in Genesis 1:26.

And straight away coming up out of the water, he saw the heavens opened, and the Spirit like a dove descending upon him. And there came a voice from heaven, saying thou art my beloved Son, in whom I am well pleased. And immediately the spirit driveth him into the wilderness. -Mark 1:9-12.

And when the devil had ended all the temptation, he departed from him for a season. And Jesus returned in the power of the Spirit into Galilee: and there went out a fame of him through all the region round about -Luke 4:13, 14.

In Chapter 22 of the book of Genesis, we see Abraham passing his 'ultimate' probation examination.

And he said, Lay not thine hand upon the lad, neither do thou any thing unto him: for now I know that thou fearest God, seeing thou hast not withheld thy son, thine only son from me -Genesis 22:12.

And the angel of the LORD called unto Abraham out of heaven the second time. And said, by myself have I sworn, saith the LORD, for because thou hast done this thing, and hast not withheld thy son, thine only son; That in blessing I will bless thee, and in multiplying I will multiply thy seed as the stars of the heaven, and as the sand, which is upon the seashore; and thy seed shall possess the gate of his enemies; And in thy seed shall all the nations of the earth be blessed; because thou hast obeyed my voice -Genesis 22:15-18.

Saul failed his 'probation' period, as the king of Israel.

And Samuel said, to Saul, Thou hast done foolishly: thou hast not kept the commandment of the LORD thy God, which he commanded thee: for now would the LORD have established thy kingdom forever.
But now thy kingdom shall not continue: the LORD hath sought him a man after his own heart, and the LORD Hath commanded him to be captain over his people, because thou hast not kept that which the LORD commanded thee -I Samuel 13: 13,14.

In Chapter 15 of I Samuel, we see how God, however, gave Saul another chance.

Unfortunately, Saul failed his 're-sit' examinations.

...Because thou hast rejected the word of the LORD, he hath also rejected thee from being king -I Samuel 15:23.

And Samuel said unto him, The LORD hath rent the kingdom of Israel from thee this day, and hath given it to a neighbor of thine, that is better than thou -I Samuel 15:28.

Our successful conduct/ passing of our 'probation' period determines our confirmation and promotion into the next level in God.

This plays a key factor whether we are to enjoy or be disqualified from the fullness of God's blessing.

But that which ye have already hold fast till I come. And he that overcometh, and keepeth my works unto the end, to him will I give power over the nations. And he shall rule them with a rod of iron; as vessels of a potter shall they be broken to shivers: even as I received of my father -Revelations 2: 25-27.

Carriers of God's glory

Blessed (empowered to prosper and exercise dominion) be the God and father of our lord Jesus Christ, who hath blessed us with all spiritual blessings in heavenly places in Christ; According as he hath chosen us in him before the foundation of the world, that we should be holy and without blame before him in love. -Ephesians 1:3, 4.

From the above, we can clearly see that our being blessed predates the existence of natural man on earth.

God proclaimed, spoke this blessing into existence (thus setting the laws of blessing into operation) when he made man (the human spirit) in Chapter One of the book of Genesis.

God blessed them (the inner man, male and female), and God said unto them, be fruitful, and multiply, and replenish the earth, and subdue it: and have dominion over the fish of the sea, and over the fowl of the air, and over every living thing that moveth upon the earth -Genesis 1:28.

A man automatically qualifies to be "the blessed of the LORD", when he makes Jesus Christ, his lord and saviour.

However, it is only when that believer exercises his faith (that comes through revelation knowledge) in this spiritual reality that he/she can come into the experiential reality of this blessing.

This is our Call: to walk in the blessing.

It is our duty, as new creation Christian believers, to manifest God's glory just like Jesus exhibited during his three and half years of Ministry.

For God who commanded the light to shine out of darkness, hath shined in our hearts, to give the light of the knowledge of the glory of God in the face of Jesus Christ (the hidden treasure). But we have this treasure in earthen (clay - referring to our humanity, weakness, flaws & imperfections) vessels, that the excellency of the power may be of God, and not of us -II Corinthians 4:6 & 7.

We are called to be stewards of His glory; manifest his light, love and life to our generation just as in the marriage feast at Galilee (John 2:1-11), where Jesus demonstrated his glory.

The beginning of miracles did Jesus in Cana of Galilee, and manifested forth his glory: and his disciples believed on him -John 2:11.

Which none of the princes of this world knew; for had they known it, they would not have crucified the lord of glory. -I Corinthians 2:8.

Also I heard the voice of the Lord, saying, whom shall I send, and who will go for us? Then said I, Here am I; send me -Isaiah 6:8.

Just like in the days of Isaiah, I believe, this is the heart cry of God: whom shall I send? Who is willing and obedient (to pay the price) to eat the good of the land (be a Carrier of my glory)?

The Spirit of God is the One who enables us to become carriers of the glory of God: wherein resides His grace, presence, anointing etc.

We can only do 'the greater works' when we become carriers of His glory.

Verily, verily, I say unto you, He that believeth on me, the works that I do shall he do also; and greater works than these shall he do; because I go unto my Father -John 14:12.

Because it is His will, we have a legal right to desire and attain to it.

The glory of this latter house shall be greater than of the former, saith the LORD of hosts; and in this place will I give peace, saith the LORD of hosts -Haggai 2:9.

Prophetically speaking, the dimensions of God's glory that will be revealed or released on the earth will surely outweigh that which was experienced by the 'early' church.

Will YOU make yourself available to God, so that you can become one of the Carriers of God's glory?

CONCLUSION

STEWARDSHIP

Most men will proclaim every one his own goodness: but a faithful man, who can find? Proverbs 20:6.

The Christian life is about being faithful to God in our stewardship of all the things He has given to us: our spirit, soul, body, finances, positions, opportunities etc.

Stewardship is the act of managing, maintaining a profitable yield or return on investment on another's property.

Our positions, wealth, experiences, education, influence should be seen as 'convertible' privileges, granted to us by God's mercies, for godly use, the furtherance of His purposes on planet earth and investing in our eternity.

Faithfulness is the key to increase and abundance.

A faithful man shall abound with blessings. -Proverbs 28:20.

We can appraise ourselves, for example in the area of Time (who or what we spend most of our time with) and money or financial resources.

Lay not up for yourselves treasures upon earth, where moth and rust doth corrupt, and where thieves break through and steal.
But lay up for yourselves treasures in heaven, where neither moth nor rust doth corrupt, and where thieves do not break through nor steal.

For where your treasure is, there will your heart be also -Matthew 6: 19 - 21.

Investing in heaven, our eternal home is supposed to be a major priority in our lives. This is true kingdom investment, of which every Christian ought to be involved in or with.
Our material and financial means should not be the basis for us, as the Church, to function as One: but our state of mind or attitude based on God's word.

The truth is that there is nothing we acquire here on planet earth that is not subject to decay. More so, you can't take it with you when you leave the earth.

It's tragic to see Christians, carnal in nature, who (for the wrong reasons) have embraced the insatiable desire for wealth, materialism, fame and position - 'the rat race'.

...the wealth of the sinner is laid up for the just -Proverbs 13:22.

Why? Is it for show off or self-aggrandizement?

I believe it is for the equitable distribution of resources.

God requires our faithfulness as stewards of His love, truth and compassion to Mankind.

These are good works, flowing out of our obedience to God, through our relationship with the Holy Spirit.

Kissing the Son is all about being relevant to God and His purposes on the earth.

It's about becoming heavenly minded/relevant to God's program and kingdom on the earth while still being a blessing to humanity.

We embrace Godly values whenever we kiss the Son.

We trust in God, whenever we kiss the Son.

We please God, whenever we kiss the Son.

So, let us all Kiss the Son: the Lord Jesus Christ ...**the Son of God, who hath eyes like unto a flame of fire, and his feet are like fine brass; -Revelations 2:18.**

www.ingramcontent.com/pod-product-compliance
Ingram Content Group UK Ltd.
Pitfield, Milton Keynes, MK11 3LW, UK
UKHW020138250726
13967UKWH00002B/728

9 781426 907821